NORTHERN LIGHTS A to Z

Mindy Dwyer

PAWS IV *published by*
SASQUATCH BOOKS

Printed in China
Published by Sasquatch Books
Distributed by Publishers Group West
12 11 10 09 08 07   9 8 7 6 5 4 3 2 1

Book design by Bob Suh

Library of Congress Cataloging-in-Publication
Data is available.

ISBN: 1-57061-515-2

Sasquatch Books
119 South Main Street, Suite 400
Seattle, WA 98104
(206) 467-4300
www.sasquatchbooks.com
custserv@sasquatchbooks.com

What Are the Northern Lights?

Many people have heard of the aurora borealis—the fantastic light show that brightens northern skies—but few understand it. As long as humans have lived in the north they have searched for meaning in the lights. Ancient legends give us many different explanations: the northern lights are a path to the afterlife, animal spirits, sky gods and goddesses, fire raining from the heavens.

In more recent times, scientists study the facts to explore how the aurora works. They have discovered many pieces of the aurora puzzle: the earth is a magnet, the sun generates wind, our atmosphere is full of electricity. They have come close to explaining this breathtaking phenomenon, but there is still plenty of mystery.

From a small jet over Fairbanks, Alaska, I watched a dancing green aurora stretch above and below the plane as far as I could see. Scientists say the northern lights begin 60 miles above the earth, but our small plane flew well below that height.

What do you think?

Even with all our scientific knowledge, there are still tales of the impossible surrounding the northern lights.

Aurora, the ancient Roman goddess of dawn, names the northern lights for a fantastic sunrise.

Borealis comes from the Latin word "boreal" which means "northern." Boreas was the Greek god of the north wind.

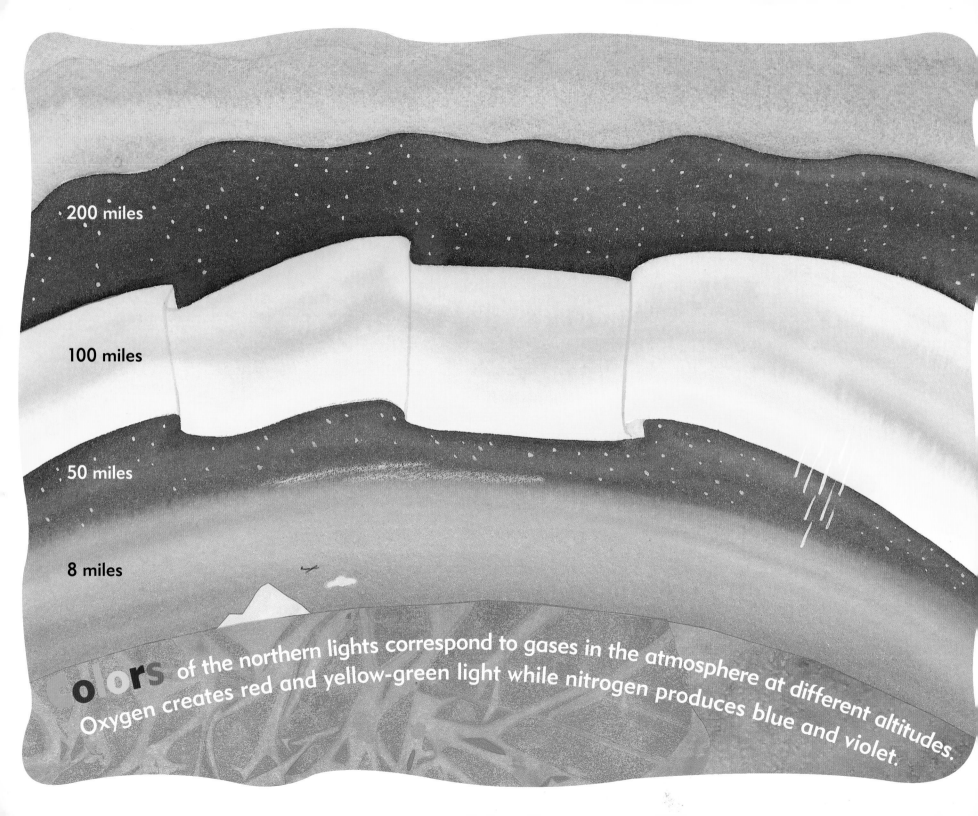

200 miles

100 miles

50 miles

8 miles

Colors of the northern lights correspond to gases in the atmosphere at different altitudes. Oxygen creates red and yellow-green light while nitrogen produces blue and violet.

Dragon

legends of ancient China and Europe originated with the red sky aurora, which people imagined to be a dragon's fiery breath flashing in the night.

Electric power surges through the northern lights. A power plant produces a few thousand megawatts compared to the aurora's one million megawatts of electricity. That's more than the total output of electric power in the United States.

Arctic Circle

Yukon River

▲
Mt. McKinley

A L A S K A

Folklore from Alaska's Lower Yukon River describes the aurora as the dance of deer, seals, salmon, and beluga whale spirits in the night sky.

Greenlanders envisioned the aurora as a ring of fires around the oceans of their homeland. The northern lights really do seem to dance like fire in an oval shape around the North Pole.

Homogeneous arcs are the quietest form of aurora. The arc can become active forming rays, bands, ribbons, spirals, and curtains. An auroral curtain seen directly overhead is called a corona.

arc

arc with rays

bands

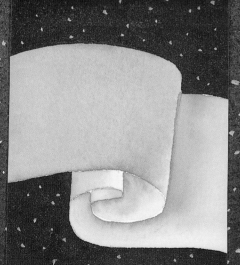

ribbon

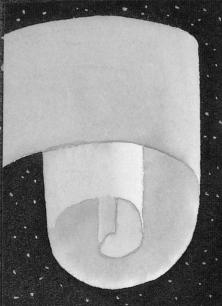

spiral

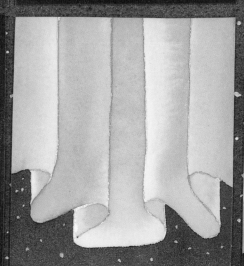

curtain

corona

Islanders of Nunivak, in the Bering Sea, tell the tale of a young boy who vanished into the northern lights—the land of walrus. When he returned he became a medicine man with the walrus as his spirit helper.

Japanese-born scientist Syun-Ichi Akasofu discovered that
aurora activity begins over the whole sky at once. Quiet curtains start
low and lighten with streaks, followed by sweeping folds or spirals
that grow brighter, move quickly, and then fade into soft cloudiness.

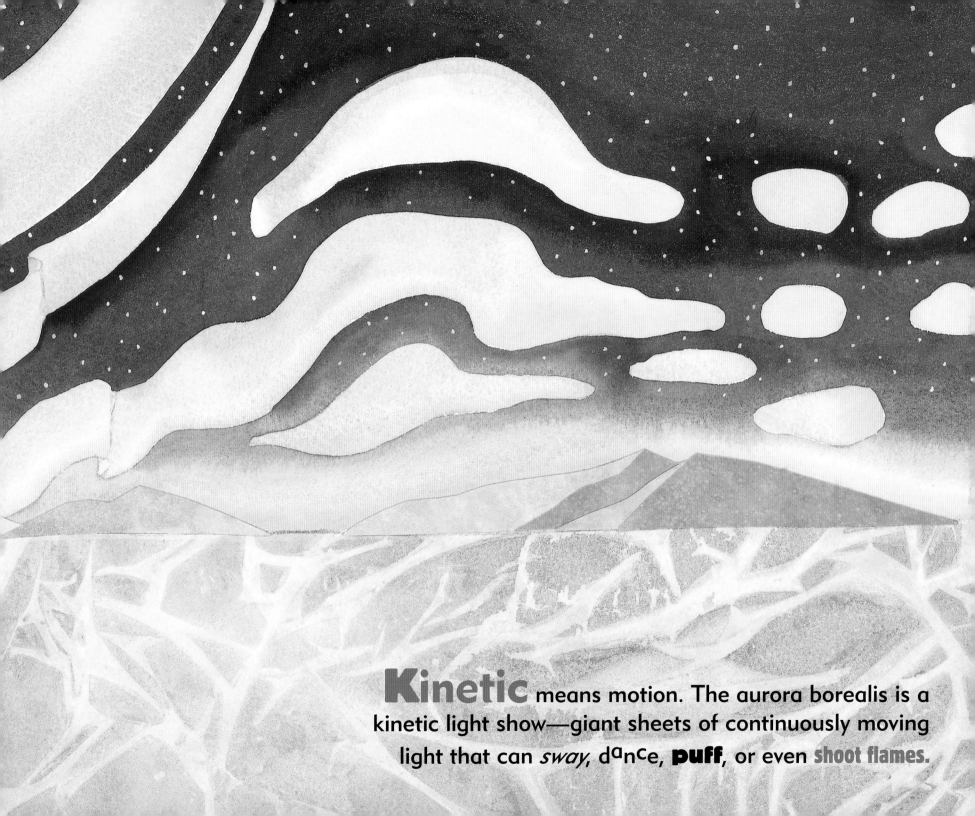

Kinetic means motion. The aurora borealis is a kinetic light show—giant sheets of continuously moving light that can *sway*, dance, **puff**, or even shoot flames.

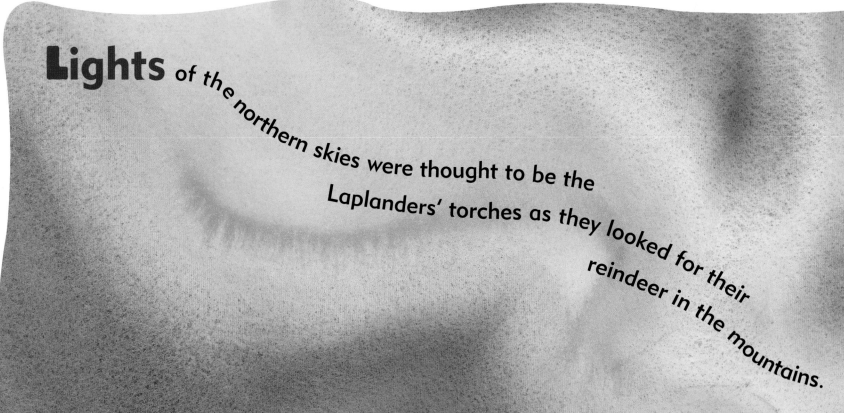

Lights of the northern skies were thought to be the Laplanders' torches as they looked for their reindeer in the mountains.

Makah people of the Pacific Northwest thought the northern lights were flaring fires from pots of whale blubber boiling in the Far North.

Northern lights have been around a long time, perhaps even before the dinosaurs. The earliest humans watched nature's awesome light show and so will the generations to come.

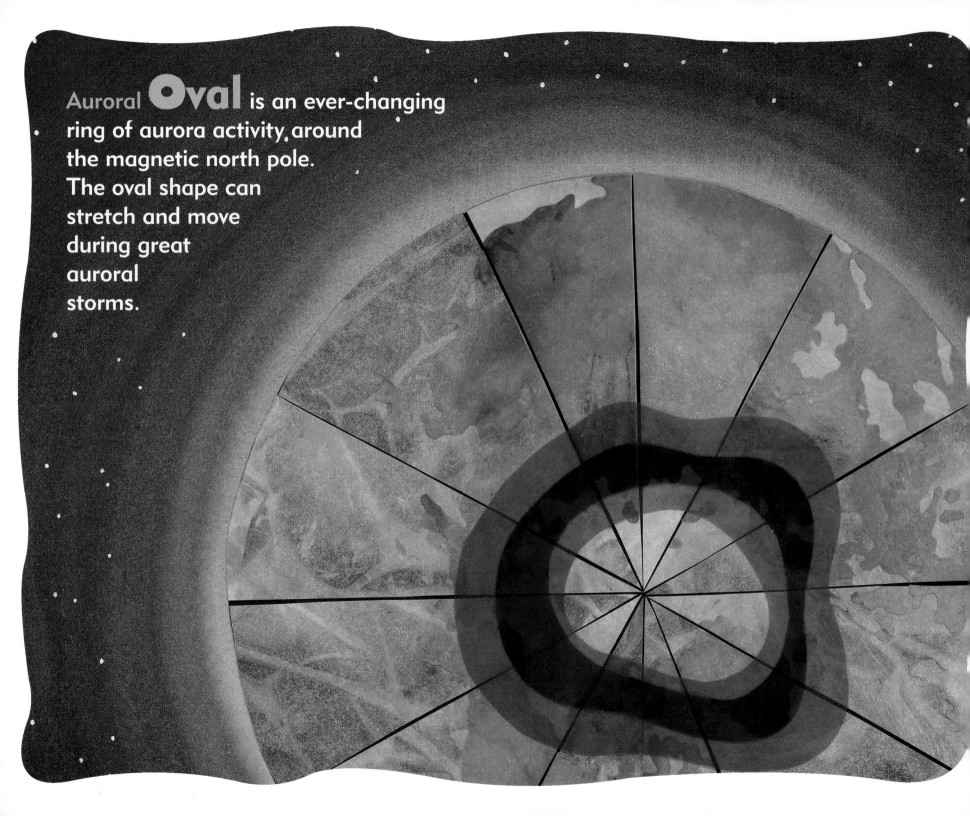

Auroral **Oval** is an ever-changing ring of aurora activity around the magnetic north pole. The oval shape can stretch and move during great auroral storms.

Powered
by its own huge
electrical current,
the aurora borealis
can disturb
radio, television,
and satellite
communications.

Quiet?

The voice of the aurora is still a great mystery. Many people have reported hearing the northern lights—tinkling bells, crackling, windy sounds—but scientists still have not explained it.

Reflections of racing swans are the northern lights of Danish folklore. As the great swans became trapped in the ice, their flapping wings created the flickering lights of the aurora.

Solar wind is a continuous stream of high-speed particles flowing out from the Sun. These electrically charged particles collide with gases in the Earth's atmosphere creating energy—the light of the aurora! Finnish myths see the Sun as Aurora's father.

Taller than you might think, the northern lights can stretch six hundred miles above the Earth, making them visible from a great distance. In 1958, a rare red aurora was seen in Mexico, several thousand miles away.

Uranus, Saturn, Jupiter, and Neptune also have auroras. Northern lights exist on planets that have an atmosphere and magnetic field.

Valkyries are beautiful warrior maidens who rode winged horses onto battlefields in Norwegian myths. The people of Norway believed the reflections from their armor caused the strange galloping light of the aurora.

"Whistle down" some say, to bring the northern lights closer. Others fear that whistling will cause the lights to swoop down and take you away forever.

Xenophanes

was a Greek philosopher who claimed that the aurora was "a gathering of moving and burning clouds." Now we know that northern lights are not actually on fire but are powered by winds from the sun.

Fort **Yukon** sits directly under the auroral oval. On clear winter nights your chances of seeing the northern lights there are 100%.

Auroral **Zones** are the places on Earth where auroras occur most often and with greatest intensity.

The Amazing Aurora

When you look at a beautiful landscape you imagine that it has always been there and always will be. It is forever. The aurora borealis is fleeting. Its lights wander across the sky, you cannot take your eyes off of them, and then suddenly they vanish! It's an experience you can feel with your whole body, an electric sensation: the hair on the back of your neck might stand up, you may smell the ozone, or hear strange, haunting sounds!

Are these experiences fact or fiction?

Syun-Ichi Akasofu, a scientist with the University of Alaska, writes, "The silence of dazzling waves of auroral light—which seem worthy of accompanying thunder—can evoke strange feelings in the viewer of the night sky."

This book presents just some of the science and myths of the aurora borealis.

I hope you will be inspired to learn more about the mysterious northern lights.

Further Reading:

Northern Lights: The Science, Myth, and Wonder of Aurora Borealis. Photography by Calvin Hall and Daryl Peterson, essay by George Bryson. Sasquatch Books, 2001.

Aurora Borealis: The Amazing Northern Lights. Written by Syun-Ichi Akasofu. Alaska Geographic Society, 1979.